KALEO

2 0 1 9

Published and distributed by The Discipleship Ministry Team, CPC
Memphis, Tennessee

The Discipleship Ministry Team of the Ministry Council of the Cumberland Presbyterian Church is the successor organization to the Board of Christian Education of the Cumberland Presbyterian Church.

Funded, in part, by your contributions to Our United Outreach.

First Edition 2019

ISBN-13: 978-1-945929-22-9
ISBN-10: 1-945929-22-7

JANUARY

S	M	T	W	T	F	S
		1	2	3	4	5
6	7	8	9	10	11	12
13	14	15	16	17	18	19
20	21	22	23	24	25	26
27	28	29	30	31		

FEBRUARY

S	M	T	W	T	F	S
					1	2
3	4	5	6	7	8	9
10	11	12	13	14	15	16
17	18	19	20	21	22	23
24	25	26	27	28		

MAY

S	M	T	W	T	F	S
			1	2	3	4
5	6	7	8	9	10	11
12	13	14	15	16	17	18
19	20	21	22	23	24	25
26	27	28	29	30	31	

JUNE

S	M	T	W	T	F	S
						1
2	3	4	5	6	7	8
9	10	11	12	13	14	15
16	17	18	19	20	21	22
23	24	25	26	27	28	29

SEPTEMBER

S	M	T	W	T	F	S
1	2	3	4	5	6	7
8	9	10	11	12	13	14
15	16	17	18	19	20	21
22	23	24	25	26	27	28
29	30					

OCTOBER

S	M	T	W	T	F	S
		1	2	3	4	5
6	7	8	9	10	11	12
13	14	15	16	17	18	19
20	21	22	23	24	25	26
27	28	29	30	31		

MARCH

S	M	T	W	T	F	S
					1	2
3	4	5	6	7	8	9
10	11	12	13	14	15	16
17	18	19	20	21	22	23
24	25	26	27	28	29	30
31						

APRIL

S	M	T	W	T	F	S
	1	2	3	4	5	6
7	8	9	10	11	12	13
14	15	16	17	18	19	20
21	22	23	24	25	26	27
28	29	30				

JULY

S	M	T	W	T	F	S
	1	2	3	4	5	6
7	8	9	10	11	12	13
14	15	16	17	18	19	20
21	22	23	24	25	26	27
28	29	30	31			

AUGUST

S	M	T	W	T	F	S
				1	2	3
4	5	6	7	8	9	10
11	12	13	14	15	16	17
18	19	20	21	22	23	24
25	26	27	28	29	30	31

NOVEMBER

S	M	T	W	T	F	S
					1	2
3	4	5	6	7	8	9
10	11	12	13	14	15	16
17	18	19	20	21	22	23
24	25	26	27	28	29	30

DECEMBER

S	M	T	W	T	F	S
1	2	3	4	5	6	7
8	9	10	11	12	13	14
15	16	17	18	19	20	21
22	23	24	25	26	27	28
29	30	31				

JANUARY

GOALS

FOCUS

SUNDAY	MONDAY	TUESDAY
		1
6	7	8
13	14	15
20	21	22
27	28	29

_____

_____

_____

_____

_____

WEDNESDAY	THURSDAY	FRIDAY	SATURDAY
2	3	4	5
9	10	11	12
16	17	18	19
23	24	25	26
30	31		

_____

_____

_____

_____

_____

_____

BIBLICAL CALL STORY: EXODUS 3:1-4:17

Moses has a very interesting call story. He encountered God in an amazing way. It is important to recall that Moses had grown up in Egypt in the palace. When he encountered God in the burning bush, he had many questions and serious reservations.

His first question was, "Who am I?" (Exod. 3:11). After prematurely and presumptuously asserting himself as a deliverer for his people in Chapter 2 and being rebuffed by a fellow-Israelite ("Who made you ruler and judge over us?" Exod. 2:14), Moses was not full of self-confidence. According to Exodus, Moses was the "meekest man on the face of the earth". To the degree that Moses' question reveals true humility, it is legitimate. But it seems that his humility is not thought out. The issue here is not who Moses is, but whose he is. God wanted to send him, and God would be with him as he was sent. Moses' authority was based upon his Divine call and the Divine presence with him as he went.

His second question was, "Who are you?" (Exod. 3:13). If Moses' authority is wrapped up in the God who has called him, then it is surely worthwhile for him to inquire as to the nature and character of God. If it were not for the next three responses of Moses, we might find this question altogether acceptable. But given what has gone on before, one would think that Moses already knew enough.

Knowing God is the highest calling of the faithful , but Moses does not seek this knowledge for himself; he seeks it because he fears that the Israelites would reject his authority. In other words, this is really a reflection of the same fears of Moses which were more openly admitted in the first question. God's answer to the first question was not sufficient for Moses, so he asked it again, in a different way. How many people "want to think it over," or "pray about it," when in reality they are reluctant to obey God's leading?

Moses' third question was, "What if they do not believe me or listen to me?" (Exod. 4:1). Is this question not a bit redundant? Moses is basically asking the same question of God for the third time. In the past, Moses doubted his calling; now he is doubting the Word of God, for the Lord has just told him, "The elders of Israel will listen to you" (Exod. 4:18). Have you ever had to face a group of skeptics and convince them that God sent you, based upon a conversation you had with a burning bush? It may seem easy to understand why Moses feared that no one would believe his story; it does seem unexplainable. In response to his question, God grants Moses the ability to perform three signs. The first two Moses performed on the spot, at God's instruction, so as to assure him. The final sign, turning water from the Nile to blood, had to wait until he was at the Nile.

In his fourth comment, he said, "But I am not eloquent!" (Exod. 4:10; cf. 6:12,30). Moses was still hung up about his own inability. Rather than acting on the basis of who the God is that called him, Moses was then retreating on the pretext that he was not a gifted communicator. This is indeed a piece of false humility. Moses clearly had no reason to trust in his own abilities, but neither should he deny the abilities which God had given him.

Moses was talking to His creator. He was saying, in effect, "God, I can't do what you ask because you did not make me well enough." While Moses was worrying about what he would say when he got to Egypt, God was spurring him to get going.

Moses was looking too far down the path. His immediate task was to get going.

Finally Moses responded, "Please send somebody else" (Exod. 4:13). Here is the bottom line. Moses did not want to go. It was not that he lacked the assurance or the authority; he simply lacked the courage to act. No reason was stated as to why God should send someone else, because Moses was all out of excuses. And so Moses plead with God for someone else to go.

God is longsuffering and patient, but according to Exodus He finally became angry. Can you imagine making God mad and then having to stand there faced with His anger? If Moses was afraid of the presence of God in the burning bush before, one can hardly imagine the fear which Moses had at this point.

God's anger was not only reflected in some visible way (did the burning bush suddenly flare up?), but it was evident in the answer which God gave to Moses (vv. 14-17). Aaron could speak fluently, so let him speak for Moses. As later events would indicate, the presence of Aaron was a burden for Moses and a stumbling block for others. Among other things, Aaron fashioned the "golden calf" and led Israel in false worship. Aaron was, at best, a mixed blessing.

In this text there are two separate threads pertaining to Moses which are intertwined. The first we might call his personal walk with God. The second we will call his public work for God. Moses' objections all deal with God's call and commission with reference to his public work. The essence of his protest was summed up in his last petition, "Please send someone else." While God graciously answered each inquiry and made provision for his concerns, we never really get to the root of Moses' problem until we come to verses 24-26.

Moses was not called and commissioned because he was so spiritual, or so successful, or because he was "ready," but because God was ready, and God would equip him to serve as he served.

The leaders whom we find portrayed in the Bible are not the giants we would like to find, but men and women whom God used in spite of their weaknesses and failures. Surely we must admit that Moses, like Elijah, was a man of "like passions", a man who had the same fears and failures as we do. It is not the greatness of the person which was the key to success, but the character of the God who calls and uses fallible people to do God's will.

We expect our leaders to succeed and always to do the right thing. Nothing in the Scriptures gives us the right to expect such perfection, either in our leaders or in ourselves. Let us look upon our leaders as those who have fears and failings like ourselves, and who need our prayers, encouragement and exhortation as much as we need theirs.

In this brief glimpse of the life of Moses, let us recognize that there are two equally dangerous extremes with regard to leadership. The first is that of being overly self-confident or too full of self-assurance. Early in his life, Moses presumptuously set out to deliver his people and ended up running for his life. That is because God had not called nor commissioned him to lead at that particular point in his life. Presumption in leadership can be deadly. The memory of that mistake might have been behind Moses' responses to God's call for him

Second, there is the danger of self-conscious passivity. This is what we see in Moses at the time when God did commission him to go to Egypt. Moses was full of all kinds of excuses why he was not the right person for the job. There are many Christians who seek to step away from leadership which God has thrust upon them.

In the final analysis, it is because they do not trust God enough to believe that much of anything can be achieved through them. It is not that they do not believe in God, it is that they do not believe that they can live up to what they believe God is calling them to do.

Regardless of the ministry which God has given, let us do so with diligence, looking first to our own walk and then to our work, trusting and obeying the "I AM" who has called us and is forever with us. The merciful thing for most of us is that God always works with, through and in spite of those who answer the call to leadership roles.

(Above comments adapted from an article on Bible.org by Rev. Bob Deffinbaugh)

DISCUSSION QUESTIONS

1. How is your story similar or different from Moses' story?

2. What questions do you have for God concerning your sense of call?

3. What do you sense God calling you to do or to be?

4. What help do you need as you begin exploring this sense of call for your life?

5. What do you think of the notion that if God calls a person, then God can and will equip that person for service.

6. What do you think about the concept that leaders who try to act before God has put a call upon them will most assuredly fail?

MODERN DAY CALL STORY: JESSICA WILKERSON

Hello, my name is Jessica Wilkerson. My husband, Reverend Patrick Wilkerson, and I are currently in the process raising support to enter the mission field in Medellin, Colombia in 2017. If you told me this 3 years ago, I would say you were crazy. If you told me this 14 years ago, I would have believed you. Our journeys can be very twisted and unpredictable! Let me share my story and my calling, and how it is still unfolding. Fourteen years ago, I was entering Bethel College (Wow! I'm old!). I was very excited and very involved in church. I can recall really understanding what it means to follow Jesus as an eighth grader in middle school. My choices and attitude noticeably changed, and I started attending church camps and mission trips consistently. During my time at Bethel, I was very involved with the campus ministry, Campus Crusade for Christ (CRU). I went on two summer long mission trips, was on the leadership team on campus, and I even was an intern at a local Baptist Church starting a college ministry. My major at Bethel was Human Services, and I just knew I wanted to help others. On the outside, it appeared that I knew exactly where my future was heading. However, my senior year, I was wrestling with my calling. I was considering being staff for the student ministry I had been so involved in, or perhaps working in a church. My experience as an intern made me decide I did not feel led to be a minister in the church. I found working in the church to be a discouraging work atmosphere, at times, and that made me question ministry all together. I also did not feel confident I could raise the financial support required to pay my salary to be campus ministry staff. I left Bethel feeling very confused and discouraged spiritually. I felt so inadequate. I did what a lot of people do when they have no clue what to do next…I went to grad school!

The fall following graduating Bethel, I entered the Master's of Social Work program at the University of TN in Nashville. I moved into an apartment with a friend from Bethel who also entered the program, and quickly obtained a serving job at The Cheesecake Factory to help pay the bills. When I first moved to Nashville, it was a huge shock. I left a small, tight knit community that you could always find someone to hang out with no matter the time of day to moving to the "big city" where I hardly knew anyone. Honestly, after leaving Bethel I was a little upset with God. I wasn't in a significant relationship that I just knew I would find in college, and I felt that I had failed at ministry also. I visited a few churches at first, but nowhere consistently. I didn't make any connections and felt like an outsider in every church that I attended. But honestly, I didn't give any of them a real chance. I made fast friends in the restaurant world, and I quickly quit attending church and distanced myself from "religion". I was going to school, had an internship, working a lot, and partying a lot.

My second year of grad school, I got the opportunity to spend a semester abroad in Monterrey, Mexico. I love traveling and adventures, so I was very excited for this opportunity. I met people from all over the world. I shared an apartment with a Canadian and a Bulgarian. The Canadian was also in the same study abroad partnership, so we spent most of our time together. We attended Spanish class with Germans, Chinese, Japanese and a Brazilian. We struggled through Mexico with our survival Spanish skills. I got the opportunity to work with the local governor's office to develop a grant for Mexicans that want to legally work temporarily in Canada and the United States. I also got to volunteer at an orphanage and learn about social issues unique to Mexico. It was truly a unique experience that I look back on fondly. We made friends with a German girl in our Spanish class, and through her we made even more Mexican friends. This is where I met Roberto.

He was a student of Ophthalmology. I started dating Roberto about mid-way through my internship. He was a very nice guy. He had roots in Catholicism but now identified as atheist. Since I had already distanced myself from religion the previous year, this was not a problem for me. Alas, my semester ended and I came home. Roberto and I decided to date long distance. So for three years, I carried on a very expensive, long distance relationship.

About three years in, we decided we had to make radical efforts to see if the relationship was going somewhere. So I moved, which was my parents' nightmare, to Brownsville, TX at the border of Mexico to be closer. I was there for exactly three months, and I was miserable. In the end, it was apparent that our religion and future plans were not congruent and we had a painful breakup.

After this breakup, in which I was convinced the relationship was going to end in marital bliss, I honestly went a little crazy. I had made him my world and my focus for three long years. I thought love was dead, and I had already given up on God awhile back. This began a lot of meaningless relationships that left me feeling even more inadequate. The lifestyle I was living became very "normal" and I thought everyone was partying and having casual sexual relationships. Yes, I went through my "wild stage" as an adult. When I was paying my own bills and had a "big girl" job. Speaking of my career, it was going well. I had graduated, and I was able to get a job immediately at a special education behavioral school working as a case manger and therapist for inner city K-7th grade kids in Nashville. It was a tough job, but I grew to love it. I felt lucky to find a job during the recession, but eventually I needed to find something that paid better. I then got a job with Youth Villages and worked as a transitional living counselor to help kids that have aged out of foster care, and then I transitioned into being a mental health mobile crisis worker for youth. I was getting great experience for my career, and I was working towards getting my license as a LCSW. I was fairly content with my career, my friends, my apartment, but not with relationships or with my spirituality. I knew I needed to come back to Jesus, but I honestly did not how to start. I decided to break it off with the guy I was currently seeing, because I knew it was not heading anywhere. I started to try out churches again. I was truly seeking God again, which it had been a long time.

Around that same time, I randomly received a Facebook message from an old boyfriend from Bethel. I hadn't talked to him in YEARS. Last time I saw him was at a funeral and he was married, but I knew he had since divorced. Honestly, I knew a lot because we had common friends. I messaged him back, and he responded almost immediately! I didn't even know what to think. We talked back and forth for a week or two. I honestly did not know his intentions. He sent a vague invitation to come to a UT basketball game in the middle of the workweek, and after consulting my sister and about three friends I decided to accept the offer to go see what this dude was all about. Plus, an old friend was also going, and I knew he could serve as a buffer. (Thanks, BJ!) I'm pretty sure he did not expect me to accept his offer, but I went and I drove back the same night to Nashville. This trip became the first of many to see Patrick and for him to come see me. We dated for three months and decided we wanted to get married, and then we married three months later. What a whirlwind! As soon as I told God I was done with being a wayward daughter, he sent Patrick and I married a minister. I moved to be with him in Knoxville, TN. My friends did not know what to think! They did not know the "religious Jessica." They just knew I met a guy, married in six months, and now was completely different. They were a little freaked out at first. My close friends have mostly stuck around, and a lot of others drifted apart from me because the only thing we had in common was our jobs or happy hour. It was a bit of a culture shock for myself, too. Yes, I had been in the church in the past, but it had been a long time ago.

I was so lucky to have a loving church and group of young adults that quickly accepted and loved on me. Patrick serves as the youth minister at Beaver Creek CPC. Since this time, Patrick and I have had two girls, and we have accepted a call to be missionaries in Medellin, Colombia. Patrick always says your call is somewhere between where your passions and faith meet. I'm very excited to use my talents and passions along with Patrick's. I hope to work with the local churches to develop and improve their social programs and also raise more awareness and educate about mental health issues. Many churches in Colombia have services such as a hot lunch program for the children in the area. This is a huge service to the struggling community. I went to Medellin, Colombia in December 2013 with Patrick and a team of young adults from the denomination.

We had the opportunity to really connect with churches in this area and meet lots of Colombian CP's. I was very humbled and excited how loved, protected, and accepted we all were by the Colombians. I do believe this trip really started the call for Patrick and I as a family to missions.

We proceeded with caution with this spark of a call, not sure if we were hearing God right. However, over the past couple of years this call has become more and more clear for us. We had many a long nights of talking and praying about this possibility. It was almost like a dripping faucet that we were no longer able to ignore. God was moving in our lives, and we had to do something about it. It was around this same time we were approached by the denomination about going into the mission field.

I am very nervous but also excited about raising our daughters, Bella and Jacqueline, in Colombia. I am very happy that I will have two bilingual girls with hopefully very fond memories of being raised in another culture. I feel very fortunate to be in an area with very loving and supportive families that we have already met in the past. I feel confident that they will take us under their wing. My call continues to unfold, and I imagine it will continue to change as life changes. I am just relieved that God's grace and forgiveness goes far beyond my understanding. He accepts us just as we are if we are willing to follow, and He leads us to the places we are called to function in His Kingdom.

What stands out to you in Jessica's call story? Can you identify with any part of her story?
What aspects of Jessica's call story gives you encouragement or frightens you when you think about your own?
Is there anything from Jessica's story that you think may help you as you consider your own sense of call?
How might you deal with your own conflicted feelings of excitement and nervousness as it relates to your sense of call?

PROJECT

As preparation for this discernment process you have been asked to complete a Spiritual Gifts Inventory. Spend some time this month going over the results of your inventory. Think about these questions.

1. Does any aspect of your results surprise you?

2. Do the results seem like a fit to you? to your mentor's knowledge of you?

3. Which of your spiritual gifts seem to match your initial concept of your call?

4. How can your identified gifts serve you through this discernment process?

FEBRUARY

GOALS		SUNDAY	MONDAY	TUESDAY
		3	4	5
		10	11	12
FOCUS		17	18	19
		24	25	26

_____

_____

_____

_____

_____

WEDNESDAY	THURSDAY	FRIDAY	SATURDAY
		1	2
6	7	8	9
13	14	15	16
20	21	22	23
27	28		

_____

_____

_____

_____

_____

_____

BIBLICAL CALL STORY: LUKE 1:26-56

In this passage we see lots of unusual, perhaps even phenomenal events taking place. In the opening verses, we learn of a young woman from Nazareth who had an encounter with Gabriel, a messenger from God. Luke tells us that Mary was perplexed by the kind of greeting that God's messenger gave her and apparently she must have shown some level of fear during the encounter, because he said to her, "Do not be afraid, Mary, for you have found favor with God." If we were to put ourselves in Mary's shoes, we could understand that a visit from an angel of God might be a bit frightening. When the angel told Mary what was to happen to her, she did not say, "Thanks for the opportunity, but I would rather not." She did not say, "Are you sure that you don't have the wrong person?" She did wonder how she could possibly conceive and bear a child as a virgin, but the angel explained how that could be accomplished. In explanation, Gabriel told her that her cousin Elizabeth, who was said to be barren, was six months pregnant. And to drive the point home that this would not be impossible for God, he said, "Nothing is impossible with God." Perhaps the most shocking part of this story is that once she understood what was being asked of her, she responded by saying, "Here I am, the servant of the Lord; let it be with me according to your word."

Shortly after her encounter with Gabriel, Mary decided to go visit her cousin Elizabeth. When Mary greeted Elizabeth, the child in her womb leapt and Elizabeth was filled with the Holy Spirit. It was as though the movement of her unborn child helped her to know that Mary was pregnant and the child whom she was carrying was to be the promised Messiah. Elizabeth honored Mary for believing the message that Gabriel had given her and for willingly agreeing to do what God had asked of her. Elizabeth recognized the magnitude of what Mary was doing, perhaps even in a way that Mary did not. Elizabeth honored Mary for agreeing to be the mother of the Lord and for her willingness to do what God had asked of her by bearing the Son of God. When Mary heard Elizabeth's words to her, she sang a song of praise because that was all that she could think to do in the realization of what was happening in her life.

The thing that sets Mary apart from others, who have experienced the call of God, is her humility in accepting God's call on her life. Mary's song extols God's faithfulness to Israel and God's desire to use the lowly of this world to bring about God's purposes. She recognized that had it not been for this child that she would bring into this world, no one other than her friends or family would ever know anything about her. But knowing the significance of this long-awaited Messiah, she knew that she would be remembered for generations to come and would even be remembered as blessed. In this song Mary also spoke of the ways that God turns things upside down in this world. The proud are scattered in the thoughts of their hearts. The powerful are brought down from their thrones. The hungry are filled with good things while the rich are sent away empty. Mary might not have fully understood all that would result from this child she would bear, but she was beginning to understand in some small part the ways that his story would change their world and she knew that it was going to turn things upside down.

1. Do you see any similarity between your story and Mary's story?

2. What do you think about Mary's willingness to believe what the messenger told her and her response to Gabriel's message?

3. How might Mary's response to her call shape your response to God's call on your life.

4. What might be the significance of Mary's visit to Elizabeth?

5. In what ways does this story impact the way that you think about your sense of call?

6. Is there some part of Mary's call or her response to that call that helps you as you think about your own sense of call?

MODERN DAY CALL STORY: CALVIN ROGERS

Watch the video of Calvin Rogers's Call Story.
www.bit.ly/2BOUn1S

1. What stands out to you from Calvin's Call Story?

2. Can you identify with any part of his story?

3. Is there any part of Calvin's story that encourages or frightens you in considering your own sense of call?

4. Who are the people in your life that you can talk to about your sense of call and who can help you to get the skills and

MARCH

GOALS		

SUNDAY	MONDAY	TUESDAY
3	4	5
10	11	12
17	18	19
24	25	26
31		

FOCUS

_____

_____

_____

_____

_____

_____

WEDNESDAY	THURSDAY	FRIDAY	SATURDAY
		1	2
6	7	8	9
13	14	15	16
20	21	22	23
27	28	29	30

_____

_____

_____

_____

_____

_____

BIBLICAL CALL STORY: ISAIAH 6

We are opening up this lesson by taking the focus off of us to turn our attention toward complete adoration of God. Isaiah 6 has long been considered the pattern for worship. It shows us that, in worship, our total attention and focus should be toward God. If truth be told, it is a rare thing for God to became our sole and complete focus. With all of the distractions in our world and as folk who pride themselves on multi-tasking, is it any wonder that we would find it challenging to focus all of our attention on one thing? Do we even think of worship as a time to focus on God or do we think of it as a time to gather with our church family to sing, pray, hear scriptures and a sermon, and perhaps anything else that we might do as a part of our worship? Do we consider the time that we spend together in corporate worship as our only worship of God or do we acknowledge other times when our focus is drawn toward God as times of worship too?

In this passage, Isaiah had to get focused on God really quickly. When one is whisked away in a vision to the position of standing before the Almighty, play time is over. It's time for serious, focused attention in the presence of God. And if you didn't know how to worship God before, it seems that once you stand before the One who is enthroned in heaven, you will learn how to praise! In Isaiah's vision, the seraphs led with words of praise.

Isaiah 6 takes us to a place that only a few have been privileged to view, even in visions. A place where we hope to reside one day, in the very presence of God. Looking at heaven through the eyes of Isaiah prepares us for the extreme holiness of God. A place where holiness supersedes everything, where we can learn to cry out with the seraphim, "Holy, Holy, Holy!" Knowing that we are a people of unclean lips also, it is somehow reaffirming to see that Isaiah's first words in God's presence were just that.

What do you think you would say if you found yourself in the very presence of God, who knows all and sees all, yet who called you before His throne?

Once Isaiah realized that he was in the presence of the Living God, he could not help but to recognize and acknowledge his own sinfulness. But the beautiful thing that happened when Isaiah confessed his sin, one of the seraphs took a live coal from the altar of incense to remove his guilt and blot out his sin. So, Isaiah showed us that when we confess our sin before God, we will be cleansed from that sin and our guilt will be purged from God's perspective. This is why some form of confession and absolution is so important in worship. Any time that we confess our sin, we can be assured that God will forgive our sin and cleanse us from unrighteousness.

After Isaiah had been forgiven, he overhead the voice of God saying, "Whom shall I send, and who will go for us?" The way that Isaiah records this statement from God is such that it does not appear to have been directed specifically at Isaiah. What a conclusion! After all that had transpired the Lord spoke up. Wings flew, voices thundered and sins were purged, but then God spoke. Not directly to Isaiah but God spoke, perhaps intentionally to be heard by Isaiah. It seemed that Isaiah just happened to overhear the question posed by God. Isaiah did not indicate that he had to ponder the question for a long time, but he does say that he responded, "Here am I; send me!" Once Isaiah realized that God had made him clean and whole, what did he do? He accepted the call of God to become a prophet. Remember that in the ancient world, the role of the prophet was to be a spokesperson for God to the people. Isaiah, who had only moments before acknowledged his identity as a man of unclean lips among a people of unclean lips, found that his lips were cleansed by the seraph and so he agreed to use his newly transformed mouth and lips to speak for God.

Do you think that God still speaks to people today? If so, is that something that can be heard audibly or do you think that God speaks in other ways? How many times do you think that has God spoken to us but His pleas have gone unheeded? Perhaps someone might say, "Well, I've never heard God speak directly to me!" God usually doesn't speak audibly, at least not in the same way that God appears to have spoken to some of the faithful from ancient times. No matter how it happens, God still speaks. One of the clearest and most trusted ways to find out what God is saying to us is to read the Bible. Another option is to listen to the promptings of the Holy Spirit when we are in prayer.

The question of the **"Lord"** was **"Whom shall I send, and who will go for us?"** **"Who"** is there that has prepared both heart and mind to follow the will of God and to go is the real question? Once Isaiah had been cleansed and had focused himself totally on God, the Lord wanted to know if Isaiah would be willing to go?

What about us? After seeing the glories of heaven and hearing of all the sights and sounds that Isaiah witnessed are we ready to respond as Isaiah did? Is it not our "reasonable service" to want to be used by the Lord? Isaiah answered the call of God on his life and he was never the same. We are today still talking about and teaching the prophecies he spoke because he said, **"Here I am; send me."** When the Lord told Isaiah what he was to say to God's people, Isaiah went forth to share that word from the Lord with the people.

1. Do you see any similarities between Isaiah's story and your own?

2. What might God be asking you to do and how can you better prepare yourself to answer God's call affirmatively?

3. What might God do through you or what might God be asking of you?

4. Have you felt a need to find ways to center yourself so that you might be better prepared to hear God's calling on your life?

5. In what ways does worship prepare us to either hear God's call or to respond to that call?

MODERN DAY CALL STORY: REV. LISA COOK

"For I was hungry and you gave me food, I was thirsty and you gave me something to drink, I was a stranger and you welcomed me, I was naked and you gave me clothing, I was sick and you took care of me, I was in prison and you visited me." ~ Matthew 25: 35-36

Street Chaplain: One who feels called to provide compassionate spiritual support, spiritual outreach, and worship and sacrament opportunities to the homeless and formerly homeless in their community.

I want to share with you where God has led me to in my call to the ministry. My personal call does not involve a typical brick and mortar church building. God has helped me to realize throughout my seminary studies and through life experiences that the congregation I should be serving are those who are experiencing homelessness and extreme poverty in Nashville, TN and the surrounding areas.

I have always felt drawn towards the pastoral care aspect of ministry. Shortly before graduating from Memphis Theological Seminary, I found myself becoming very involved with the homeless community in my area through a series of unique events. For example, I was asked in April of 2013, to serve on the Board of Directors for The Contributor, a street paper in Nashville that is sold by vendors who are experiencing homeless or were formerly homeless. Suddenly I found myself working with a group of people I had never considered to be a part of my call or future ministry.

Street Chaplaincy is a new concept in ministry. In many ways, a Street Chaplain is much like a local pastoral care missionary who ministers to and provides spiritual outreach to a community of people who are often forgotten or ignored, and who relies on donations to support the work they have been called to by God.

I was ordained in November 2013 in the Cumberland Presbyterian Church as a street chaplain to the homeless community in the Nashville area, and became the founder of "Sacred Sparks Ministry". In the winter Sacred Sparks organizes an emergency warming shelter in a Cumberland Presbyterian Church to provide shelter, food and basic necessities for up to 24 adults per night. Through the donations of the building, cots, clothes and food, this ministry has been able to protect some of the lives of those without homes in Nashville.

However, the work and the call extend beyond just the winter months. Every Wednesday there's the group trip to the laundry center to allow people to wash their clothes, with transport and quarter donations provided by Sacred Sparks volunteers. There's transport provided to allow trips to visit family members, support to attain identification cards, and Bible studies in the park, and a program called Faith and Fitness that focuses on spiritual and physical fitness for friends who have recently been housed.

Providing for the physical and material needs of the friends that I serve through this call may be important, but it is the last of the four Sacred Sparks' goals:
(1) Being present and building relationships with our friends in the homeless community.
(2) Providing real opportunities for spiritual growth through worship, study, and pastoral care.
(3) Providing two-way educational opportunities to help build relationships and community.
(4) Providing outreach and basic necessities for survival, shelter, and well-being.

Though this unique call and this ministry is based in the tented communities throughout the city rather than a church, make no mistake here, the friends I serve who are experiencing homelessness and extreme poverty ARE my congregation, and I AM their pastor. Like all congregations they need the love and support of a community but they are also invited to become disciples and serve in the body of Christ.

Rev. Lisa Cook
Street Chaplain, Sacred Sparks Ministry

1. What stands out to you in Lisa's call story?

2. Can you identify with any part of her story?

3. What aspects of Lisa's call story gives you encouragement or frightens you when you think about your own?

4. Is there anything from Lisa's story that you think may help you as you consider your own sense of call?

5. Do you find comfort in knowing that it was not until Lisa was nearly done with her seminary training that she discovered what direction her call would take?

PROJECT

One aspect of Kaleo is that you will develop a project that might help you through this discernment process. Perhaps that will take the form of some type of Christian service or perhaps it will be an opportunity to shadow a person whose ministry is similar to what you perceive to be a calling that God is placing upon your heart. Perhaps your project will take the form of engagement in some aspect of ministry in your local congregation or within your presbytery. Your project may involve some service industry or other career path which you need to explore in some way. Take some time this month to talk with your mentor and brainstorm ideas of what you might do in the way of a project that would help you to get a clearer sense of God's calling on your life.

APRIL

GOALS

FOCUS

SUNDAY	MONDAY	TUESDAY
	1	2
7	8	9
14	15	16
21	22	23
28	29	30

WEDNESDAY	THURSDAY	FRIDAY	SATURDAY
3	4	5	6
10	11	12	13
17	18	19	20
24	25	26	27

_____

_____

_____

_____

_____

_____

BIBLICAL CALL STORY: ACTS 8:26-40

Philip obeyed Jesus' instructions. He left Jerusalem and went to Samaria to preach the Good News. Crowds of people saw God's power working through Philip and when they heard the Good News about Jesus they believed in Him. Because Philip obeyed Jesus' instructions many lives were changed in Samaria. They heard the Good News about Jesus and believed in Him.

While in Samaria, the angel of the Lord instructed Philip to go south to the road-the desert road-that goes down from Jerusalem to Gaza. According to Acts, Philip received those instructions and did not hesitate to obey. He immediately obeyed this message from God. He didn't ask questions or argue with God. He didn't tell God he would do it later, he went immediately where God told him to go. You will note that one difference in this call story is that Philip was already working as a teacher and evangelist when he received this particular call. It is also significant that this call to action on Philip's part was for a very specific instruction of a place to go, but there was no indication as to what he was to do once he got out on that road from Jerusalem to Gaza.

What do you think your response might be if you believed that God was giving you such vague instructions about what God wanted you to do other than to go to a particular location? Do you think you would obey immediately or do you think you might make excuses or in some other way delay your obedience to God's instructions? Would you try to get more details about what was being asked of you?

It's important to stop and think about how to recognize if God has clearly instructed us to do something for God. Has there ever been a time when you felt that God clearly spoke to you and told you what to do? Sometimes people think that God only spoke to the people in the Bible. Some people might think that God only speaks to adults? But there is strong evidence in the Bible that shows us that God spoke people of all ages. In the Old Testament there is the story of Samuel, who was still a young boy when God spoke to him. There is also evidence that God spoke to people of advanced years. Can you think of older persons from the Bible who heard a message from God?

No matter how old we are, how would we ever know if the God of the universe is speaking to us? Clearly the number of people who have received audible instructions from God is relatively low, but there are many other ways that God chooses to speak to people: through other persons, through events, through the church and through the Bible. Whatever we think God may be saying to us would have to be in agreement with what the Bible teaches.

Think about this story of Philip and imagine if God told us to approach a vehicle and join the person inside it how we might respond. How do you think you might respond to that kind of an instruction from God? If God actually told us to do that we would definitely need to pray for courage and strength to approach a stranger! Maybe Philip did that as he approached the chariot. We don't know because it's not recorded in the Scriptures.

Approaching the chariot Philip heard the Ethiopian reading out loud from the prophet Isaiah. Do you ever read God's Word out loud? Philip is such an exciting example as an obedient follower of Jesus! Because Philip was open to this request from God, he had the opportunity to talk with the Ethiopian man about Jesus. Sometimes God prompts us to share with someone and they don't even seem to hear what is being said. Sometimes we share the Good News and the person says

'I have wanted to know who this Jesus character was and what his life was all about, but no one has told me about him'.

Philip had the opportunity to share Jesus fly open when the Ethiopian said, "How can I understand unless someone explains it to me?" Thankfully, Philip was following Jesus and obeyed His instructions. He had wisdom to see that this man was truly seeking God. When he was invited to sit in the chariot he immediately accepted.

The Ethiopian turned to Philip and said, "Tell me, please, who is the prophet Isaiah talking about, himself or someone else?" Philip began to talk with the man about that passage and how it was a prophecy that referenced Jesus. He tried to share all of the important information about the Good News of Jesus Christ.

Because Philip explained the Scriptures to that man he finally understood. He saw some water and asked, "Why shouldn't I be baptized?" Some translations or versions of the Bible leave verse 37 out. Acts 9:37 contains the following words, "Then Philip said, "If you believe with all your heart, you may." And he answered and said, "I believe that Jesus Christ is the Son of God."

The Ethiopian gave orders for the chariot to stop. He and Philip climbed out. Philip took the Ethiopian man down to the water and baptized him and the man went on his way rejoicing.

1. With which of the two characters in this passage do you most closely identify? Do you see yourself as a seeker like the Ethiopian? Do you see yourself more as Philip who was already doing God's work, but who perceived a call to a specific task for God?

2. What is the significance of the detail in the story that the Ethiopian had traveled to Jerusalem to worship and was headed back home?

3. Are there aspects of this story that surprise or confuse you?

4. What other aspects of this story seem relevant to you as you try to discern your call?

5. How do we know what God's instructions to us are?

6. Many modern Bible students look at a Scripture text and one of the first questions they ask is, "What does this verse mean to me?" While that is a valid question, it might not be the student's first question in studying a passage. When studying God's Word, one might start by asking, Who is speaking? Who is being addressed? What is the context of the passage? Under what historical setting did this take place? Is this text history, prophecy, poetry, or some other kind of scripture? After we discover the original intention of the writer, then we might be better prepared to ask, "What does this mean to me?"

7. Do you see any similarities in this story and your own life story?

8. How does this call story impact your own sense of call?

MODERN DAY CALL STORY: REV. TROY GREEN

Maybe it was perfectionism, but in my teens I realized that I could not do better with my life than to do what God wanted. God not only knows everything about everything, but God wants what is best for us. So, it has been my practice to seek God's direction throughout my life. This is not to say that I've always responded rightly to God's directions! But God is good--even to the fearful, foolish and stubborn.

In college my future wife asked me if I was going to be a pastor. She was herself a Preacher's Kid and knew firsthand the difficulties and hardships of congregational ministry. Church members think they own a piece of you, family gets set to the back in order "To do the Lord's work", and ministers often move frequently. I told her, "I have no interest, inclination, nor desire to be a pastor, but if God calls me to it, I'm going."

I wish I could say it was simply my great faith that made me so hungry and willing to follow God's lead, but underneath it was mostly fear of making a mistake and trying to win God's approval. As I prayed over my future profession and wavered between pastoring and counseling, I sensed a disconcerting impression to be a missionary.

I put it out of my mind. I can barely manage English and to learn another language seemed impossible. High school and college classes in Spanish provided the evidence. Then, there was the living out of the country and away from family. I tried not to hear it, but that quiet Voice works around our attempts to ignore it. Finally, it dawned on me how foolish it was for me to resist God's guidance. So then, fear and all, I said, "Lord, if You want me to be a missionary, I will be." I expected doors would start opening and God would start confirming the call. Instead, I immediately sensed God communicate, "No, I'm not calling you to be a missionary. I'm just showing you your willingness to follow."

After that, I felt God leading me more and more toward psychology and maybe a future in the mental health field. Along the way, I would preach from time to time. It was fun, and I could see God was in it, but it seemed a temporary thing. I graduated Maryville College with a major in Clinical Psychology and got married that summer. Within four years, I realized I needed a Master's Degree to be licensed as a counselor so I enrolled at MTSU. Long story short, halfway through I had to drop out because the time demands and my difficulties administering IQ tests made it impossible. I felt defeated.

I started praying and asking God where I went wrong. I requested catalogues from other schools and seminaries. I can't detail how profoundly the failure affected me. I questioned everything, especially my judgment and obedience. The crisis actually led me to say a prayer like this, "Lord, I can't tell up from down. I don't trust my judgment, but I want to hear what you want me to do. So make it clear. Make it so clear that I can't miss it. Even if You have to show me in a dream or something. If You will show me, I will do it." That prayer had faith.

That night—surprise, surprise—I had a dream. In the dream I was in the hall of a small house with a blank wall in front of me. I had a pencil that was about two feet long. Behind me I heard a voice say, "Write MA," on the wall. I did. The voice said, "Draw a line through it." I marked it right in half. Then one more command, "Write MMFT." Although it was just 4:00 a.m., I immediately woke up and asked myself, "What the heck is MMFT?"

That afternoon when I got home from work I had a white envelope with the catalog from Trevecca Nazarene University. And right in the middle was a degree program for Master of Marriage and Family Therapy: an "M.M.F.T.!"

I thought that was the coolest thing. The M.A. from MTSU was 45 credit hours, and I thought this would be the same. It was not. It was 51 credit hours. My excitement evaporated in anger, and I threw the catalogue down. I don't have time for that!

A day or so later it dawned on me that I could transfer in my 24 credit hours from MTSU. I was again happy and excited. I got home and found in the catalogue they would only accept 9 hours of transfer credit. Bam! I threw that little white book across the table again.

This went on for a couple of weeks back and forth with me thinking of solutions and only finding more problems. It was going to be three times as expensive, take a year and a half longer to graduate, and I would have to drive twice as far. No way.

The thing was that during this time I was waking up every morning at 4:00 a.m. fully alert. I would just wake up. My wife is a light sleeper so even though I didn't move she would wake up when I woke up. After two weeks she asked in exasperation, "What is wrong with you?" I started to defend myself and say I didn't know, and then my own words came back to me, "Lord, if you show me I will follow."

That afternoon I sent in my application. Over the next few weeks, I started to learn other things. Yeah, it was twice as far, but I only had to go half as often. Yes, I needed to take more classes, but the way they did block scheduling I would only be graduating one semester later than if I had stayed at MTSU. At this point I was going regardless of the obstacles, but it was encouraging to see. Plus, we started sleeping past 4:00 a.m.!

Then the Friday before I was supposed to start classes my boss called me in the office to give me an unexpected raise. Honestly, it was the exact difference in the cost of tuition plus an extra $60 a month which would cover book expenses.

PART TWO

Currently, I have two careers. I have a counseling practice in Fayetteville, and I'm a part time minister at Petersburg. I'd like to say I was more obedient answering my call to ordained ministry, but it's not true. Over and over again my fear and my "need to understand" have interfered with my feet. God has had to tell me that if He is big enough to tell me what to do then He's big enough to take care of me if I make a mistake. He's reminded me that perfection is not required. God even helped me accept that He can lead me even if I don't know enough to cooperate. Our God is big!

In 1999 my wife's home church (Petersburg) had a minister in poor health, and he asked if I would preach at least one Sunday a month. God gave the go ahead. Then the pastor wanted me to do every other week. We thought God was leading, so we agreed even though we had a three-year-old and lived an hour and a half away. Within a couple of months, the minister retired and we found ourselves driving down every Sunday.

I told the congregation I would serve until they found a real preacher, and they winked at me and said, "Sure, we'll get right on it." Eventually, God would indicate that it was ok for me to continue. Then, late in 2004 my wife started asking if I thought God was calling us to move closer to Petersburg. With great piety I ignored her and stuffed my ears with cotton. God got through anyway, and in early 2005 I opened a counseling office in Fayetteville, and we moved there in the fall.

The call to ordained ministry has been a much more gradual call. Maybe God knew that if my wife recognized it was coming then she would bolt, or maybe I would too so the Lord used an incremental call.

I should also point out that for a married couple, God's call to ministry is going to involve both of them. I knew a man who disregarded his wife and the counsel of several wise ministers to venture into a traveling revival ministry without his wife being on board. I'm convinced that if God is calling one person in a marriage then God is not going to leave the other behind.

So now, I find myself with a full time counseling practice and serving as Petersburg's minister. While I felt called to serve here (and later invited to seek ordination to better meet the church's need), I believe God left it to me regarding PAS or seminary. That and many other things have helped me come to see that ministry is an interactive activity. Yes, God wants obedience when He directs, but God doesn't speak on everything because God also gives us gifts, interests, and abilities that we can bring to the equation. We were not created to be mindless obedient robots but to live in a vibrant interactive relationship with God.

And God's calls have continued. A few years ago, I felt the Lord prompt me to get more involved on a denominational level. Soon after, Robert Heflin asked me to complete a Personal Information Form, and I wound up on the Ministry Council. I had to look up what that was! Recently, God has shared a vision to revolutionize the way our denomination functions. It's the most daunting and exciting call so far.

II Chronicles 16:9a states, "For the eyes of the Lord move to and fro throughout the earth that He may strongly support those whose heart is completely His." God has a purpose for each of us and will supply the grace to fulfill them. I'm less intimidated by my inadequacies than I used to be. Perfection really is not required. I've come to understand that its more about God than me—the outcomes are in God's hands, my part is obedience. As my favorite poem says, "And I am learning to shut up and pedal in the strangest places...with my delightful constant companion, Jesus Christ." Regardless of the adventure to which God calls you, may you experience the same.

Grace,
H. Troy Green

1. What stands out to you from Troy's Call Story?

2. Can you identify with any part of his story?

3. Is there any part of Troy's story that encourages or frightens you in considering your own sense of call?

4. How do you feel about the prospect of turning your life over to God to lead you in the direction that God desires for you?

1. What stands out to you from Troy's Call Story?

PROJECT

As you continue to think about a project, perhaps it might help to think about educational requirements that would be needed to pursue the calling that you are perceiving. Maybe your project could be related to looking at educational options and paths that might be related to your call. Spend some more time thinking about some options for a project that will help you through this discernment process.

NOTES

MAY

GOALS

FOCUS

SUNDAY	MONDAY	TUESDAY
5	6	7
12	13	14
19	20	21
26	27	28

_____

_____

_____

_____

_____

WEDNESDAY	THURSDAY	FRIDAY	SATURDAY
1	2	3	4
8	9	10	11
15	16	17	18
22	23	24	25
29	30	31	

_____

_____

_____

_____

_____

_____

According to Acts, Saul was a zealous Jew and not only that, he saw it as his mission in life to help stop the Followers of the Way, those who professed faith in Jesus Christ. He had been relentless in his pursuit to stop those who professed faith in Jesus Christ. He was so determined to help the Jews to stamp out Christianity, that he asked for permission from the High Priest to search throughout Damascus to find those who were followers of the Way so that he could gather them up, bind them and bring them back to Jerusalem to stand trial. He was passionate about his calling to defend his faith and he wanted to help further the cause of Judaism.

As he traveled to Damascus, he was struck blind by a bright light and he heard a voice asking him, "Saul, why do you persecute me?" Saul asked who was asking the question and the reply came, "I am Jesus, whom you are persecuting. Get up and enter the city, and you will be told what you are to do." The writer said that those who were traveling with him heard the voice, but saw no one, so they were confused. When Saul got up from the ground, he could see nothing even though his eyes were open. So, his travel companions had to lead him by the hand into Damascus. The scriptures said that he neither ate nor drank for three days as he waited in blindness for another message to come to him. One might wonder what was going on inside Saul's head as he sat for three days fasting in darkness. Because he was a devout Jew, he was likely prayerful. Being the Hebrew scholar that he was, he could have been reflecting on scripture passages that were formative for him or that he had memorized. He could have had some of his travel companions reading to him. We have no real way of knowing all that he did during those three days other than wait for further instructions and pray.

The disciple Ananias, who was living in Damascus, heard the Lord call to him from a vision and he answered, "Here I am, Lord." The Lord told Ananias to get up and go to the house of Judas on Straight Street to find Saul from Tarsus who had received a vision from God. The vision was that Ananias would come to him and lay hands on him to restore his sight. Clearly, Ananias had heard of Saul and his persecution of the Followers of the Way. It would only seem natural that he would be afraid to go to offer help to Saul. He was aware of what Saul had done to followers in Jerusalem and he was aware that Saul had the authority of the chief priests to capture followers in Damascus in order to return them to Jerusalem. Is it any wonder that Ananias was hesitant to go looking for Saul of Tarsus to help him regain sight?

The Lord assured Ananias that God's plan was to convert Saul of Tarsus. Not only did God plan to convert Saul, but God intended to make him an instrument to bring the name of Christ to the Gentiles, to kings and before the people of Israel. Ananias was even further assured by the news that God intended to show Saul how he must suffer for the sake of Christ. Apparently those words of assurance were sufficient to convince Ananias, because he went to that house, laid hands on Saul. He told Saul that he knew what had happened to him on the road and he had been sent there by Jesus to help him regain his sight and be filled with the Holy Spirit. The author said that immediately something like scales fell from his eyes and his sight was restored. Once he was able to see again, he got up and was baptized and after eating he regained his strength. The writer said that he spent a few days in Damascus with the disciples of Jesus, then Paul began to share the Gospel of Jesus Christ in the synagogues.

1. Describe both the calls in this story. How were they different and how were they similar?

2. With which of these two men do you most closely identify?

3. What, if any, similarities do you find to your own sense of call?

4. How does this call story encourage you?

5. How does this call story challenge you?

MODERN DAY CALL STORY: BRITTANY SPRADLING

When I was in high school, I remember riding down the road with my mom on Edmondson Pike in my hometown of Nashville, TN. I have no idea where we were headed, but I remember exactly where I was in that moment. I happened to look up at myself in the passenger mirror, and my heart knew - I was being called for something bigger. I'm sure my calling, even at that time, was not a one moment occurrence, but it was more like a rocket building up over time to the actual point in which the engine ignites and takes off into space. At the time, my heart was leading me into full-time youth ministry. I'm not sure I was following the wrong path, even though it's not where my call has taken me today. Perhaps it was God preparing my heart to be married to a youth minister. I can say for certain, the call was so strong that I started researching schools in which I could learn more.

I took off to Asbury College, now Asbury University, in Wilmore, KY. I met several interesting people with a variety of interesting calls. My eyes were opened to the wealth of ways in which I could be involved in ministry and was blessed to be involved in a junior high ministry through a congregation in Lexington, KY. After completing my first year at Asbury, I learned of an internship position that was developed by the Christian Education Board of my home church, Tusculum CP Church. Since I was too close in age to many of the youth, it was decided by the Board that I could intern in children's ministry. This was my first real experience in working with children and their families, and I fell in love.

After the summer, I returned to Asbury for one semester but was quite unsettled being there. I transferred back to Nashville to complete my college career at Belmont University. Once back home, I began volunteering with the children's ministry at Tusculum as a volunteer. I helped out with our Wednesday night program and started a drama/music/arts program that I named Angelic C.H.A.O.S. I quickly found myself spending more time working with the children and families than I did at college or my paying part-time retail position. Also, I began dating the new youth minister brought on at Tusculum.

At Belmont, I looked to find a major close to the Christian Ministries major I was pursuing at Asbury; however, the closest was a major in Religion, which did not seem to be the right fit. I decided to major in Psychology and minor in Youth Ministry and Church Recreation. I chose this minor because I knew it would keep me close to learning from others who were ministering in various ways at local churches. One of my classes allowed for ministers and leaders to come speak about their current ministries. There was one married couple who came to speak to the group. They were each serving in full-time ministry in separate congregations. They acknowledged the struggles for their marriage and children. After hearing them speak, I became quite conflicted regarding my calling into full-time children's ministry and dating a man who was already in full-time youth ministry. I knew I did not want to raise a family with two church homes. Our church community was not big enough to have both a full-time youth minister and a full-time children's minister, and our youth ministry was absolutely flourishing. It was then I knew lay ministry was my call, and maybe it had been my call all along.

After two years at Belmont, I graduated. My first two full-time jobs were in the social work field, one specifically focused on children diagnosed with a major mental illness and the second with Big Brothers Big Sisters of Middle TN, interviewing children and adults for the program and making matches. I was in social work for four years. During my time in social work, I learned more about schools, families, children, and the judicial system than any book or teacher could have taught. In my personal life, I married the youth minister, had a beautiful girl and we had another baby girl on the way. With all the moving parts in my personal life, coupled with serious safety concerns in my career, I knew I needed to make a change.

I began work for a clinical drug research organization in data management. It was a total 180 from my previous career. I travelled the world and learned so much about other cultures. I also found the structure of the job allowed me to know I would be free to continue my ministries in the church. Two years ago, I began working in my family's company, helping manage health insurance, pharmacy and wellness plans. The change has helped my lay ministry to grow even further. I have more flexibility and understanding when I need to take a day off for ministry, community meetings and events. I also have more time to devote to my own children.

Since the time I realized God was calling me into something deeper than having my name on a church roll, life has continued to grow around this constant call to be a lay leader. Like the branch of a vine, I've undergone small, precise cuts to make room for new growth, amazing relationships and experiences. Sometimes these cuts hurt, but oh, the beauty that remains and the beauty that replaces. In this growth, I've learned how important it is to listen instead of talk and follow instead of lead, to breathe and to rest. I cannot say many things for certain, but this I know, I was called to be a lay leader.

1. What stands out to you from Brittany's Call Story?

2. Can you identify with any part of her story?

3. Is there any part of Brittany's story that encourages or frightens you in considering your own sense of call?

4. Brittany quickly identified a need for educational training to explore her sense of call. What educational opportunities will you need to explore your call more fully?

5. How do you feel about how her sense of call changed over the years from youth ministry to lay ministry?

PROJECT

If you are still undecided on a project for this year, you need to spend more time talking with your mentor about what ideas you have for a project during this year of discernment. If you have determined what you want to do as your project, you need to work on your goals and plans for the project. You also may need to work on identifying people or resources that you may need in order to actually do your project. Bear in mind that the goal is for this to be an ongoing project, but which you could complete by late October or early November. If the two of you are at a loss for ideas about what kind of a project to do, you might talk with your minister or youth leader. Know that a part of the immersion experience in July is to talk about your project ideas, so if you are still undecided or have uncertainties in July, Melissa Malinoski or Nathan Wheeler will be happy to help you to come up with some ideas for your project. It will just be very helpful for you to spend time thinking about it each month until you figure out what it is that you might want to do.

NOTES

JUNE

GOALS

FOCUS

SUNDAY	MONDAY	TUESDAY
2	3	4
9	10	11
16	17	18
23	24	25
30		

WEDNESDAY	THURSDAY	FRIDAY	SATURDAY
			1
5	6	7	8
12	13	14	15
19	20	21	22
26	27	28	29

_____

_____

_____

_____

_____

_____

NOTES

JULY

GOALS

FOCUS

SUNDAY	MONDAY	TUESDAY
2	3	4
9	10	11
16	17	18
23	24	25
30		

_____

_____

_____

_____

_____

_____

WEDNESDAY	THURSDAY	FRIDAY	SATURDAY
			1
5	6	7	8
12	13	14	15
19	20	21	22
26	27	28	29

_____

_____

_____

_____

_____

_____

AUGUST

GOALS	SUNDAY	MONDAY	TUESDAY
	4	5	6
	11	12	13
FOCUS	18	19	20
	25	26	27

WEDNESDAY	THURSDAY	FRIDAY	SATURDAY
	1	2	3
7	8	9	10
14	15	16	17
21	22	23	24
28	29	30	31

_____

_____

_____

_____

_____

_____

BIBLICAL CALL STORY: RUTH 1 & 2

Ruth's story is very unusual. She was a Moabite woman, who married an Israelite man. Marrying outside the faith was frowned upon heavily among Israelites. Knowing what we know about the Hebrew people, it is shocking that one of the two books of the Hebrew Bible that bears the name of a woman would be a woman who was not born an Israelite. Let's look more closely at her story.

Elimelech and Naomi, along with their sons, Mahlon and Chilion, moved to Moab because of a famine in Judah. Apparently life in Moab was better than life in Judah, so they stayed there. Elimelech died, but his wife and sons continued to live in Moab and her sons even married Moabite women. Given the way that Israelites felt about intermarriage with people outside of Israel or Judah, this is a shocking thing. While Naomi may have wanted to return home to Judah, she would never have considered that as long as her sons were living in Moab, because it would have been their duty as sons to provide for her. Sadly, both of her sons died and that left three widows with no man to provide for them. In the ancient world, women would have had virtually no way to provide for themselves.

It seems that Naomi had close relationships with her two Moabite daughters-in-law. After both of Naomi's sons died, she made the decision to go back to Judah because she had heard that the famine was over and times were better there. Both daughters-in-law thought they should go with her. Naomi insisted that they return to their own families and their own gods as she was planning to do. Orpah returned to her family, but Ruth insisted that she stay with Naomi and go to Judah to make a new life. We are not given a clear indication as to why Ruth would do such a thing. Perhaps it was devotion to Naomi, who had been like a mother to her. Perhaps it was that she knew how difficult Naomi's life would be without a husband or sons to provide for her. Perhaps Ruth had worshiped the God of Judah with her husband and family long enough that she wanted to remain a part of that faith community. What other possible motives could have prompted Ruth to leave her homeland and travel with Naomi to Judah?

During my parent's generation, the words which Ruth said to Naomi were often used in wedding ceremonies. There was even a popular wedding song entitled, "Whither Thou Goest". When we read this story, we recognize that Ruth's words, "Where you go, I will go; where you lodge, I will lodge; your people shall be my people, and your God my God." were words from a daughter-in-law to her widowed mother-in-law. While they are a beautiful statement of commitment between two people, using them for marriage is taking them out of their original context.

For our purposes, it seems that those words are a recognition on Ruth's part that her mother-in-law, Naomi, needed her to try to help provide for Naomi. Ruth went with Naomi to Judah and worked in the ways that she could to sustain both of them. Once they were in Judah, Naomi and Ruth had few options for survival, so Ruth went to glean in the fields behind the harvest workers. It was there that Ruth found favor with one of Elimelech's relatives, a man by the name of Boaz. He told his workers to allow her to glean behind them, because he knew what she was doing for Naomi. Apparently he had heard about her sacrifice of leaving her family to look after and support Naomi. He was impressed by her willingness to move to Judah and help her mother-in-law, so he eventually encouraged his workers to intentionally leave more for her to glean behind them.

It is important to know that in the ancient Israelite culture, male family members were expected to help the widows of their next of kin. As a matter of fact, the Law of Moses laid out specific guidelines for marrying the widow of one's next of kin and providing for them an heir to carry on the family line. In time, Boaz did marry Ruth and they had a son named Obed, who was the father of Jesse and the grandfather of King David. Through this child, Naomi and Ruth were restored because they had a male child to carry on the family line.

1. What stands out to you in Ruth's call story?

2. Do you see any similarities between her story and yours?

3. What lessons are there in Ruth's story which will inform your own sense of call?

4. Do you wonder about sacrifices that you may have to make in order to answer your call?

5. How would you feel if God's call on your life led you away from home and family?

MODERN DAY CALL STORY: DREW GRAY

Watch the video of Drew Gray's Call Story.
www.bit.ly/2rh6nmN

1. What stands out to you from Drew's Call Story?

2. Can you identify with any part of his story?

3. Is there any part of Drew's story that encourages or frightens you in considering your own sense of call?

4. How do you feel about the fact that even after answering a call to ministry, there may be a change in the direction Drew's call took over time?

5. What might this idea of changing calls say about how you move forward in the exploration of your sense of call?

PROJECT

Spend some time thinking about your project, if you still need to do that. If you are closer to choosing a specific project, you might think about some of the resources that you will need to work toward this project.

NOTES

66

SEPTEMBER

GOALS

FOCUS

SUNDAY	MONDAY	TUESDAY
1	2	3
8	9	10
15	16	17
22	23	24
29	30	

_____

_____

_____

_____

_____

WEDNESDAY	THURSDAY	FRIDAY	SATURDAY
4	5	6	7
11	12	13	14
18	19	20	21
25	26	27	28

_____

_____

_____

_____

_____

_____

BIBLICAL CALL STORY: JOHN THE BAPTIZER, LUKE 1:5-25, 57-80, LUKE 3:1-22

The call of John the Baptist began with messenger visits to his parents. Zechariah was a priest and he had devoted his life to the faith. He and his wife, Elizabeth, were childless and were past their prime child-bearing years. In the ancient world the blame for childlessness was placed predominantly on the woman, because she was viewed as barren. It would appear that this couple had not completely given up their hopes for a child, because it seems that they continued to pray for a child. Surely they were coming to terms with the idea that their window of opportunity was rapidly slipping away. Yet Luke referred to both of them as righteous.

As Zechariah was in the sanctuary to offer the incense offering, an angel of the Lord appeared to him. Clearly Zechariah was afraid, even terrified. Notice how every time a messenger from God approaches human beings, they become scared. That does not seem far-fetched. If we were to be approached by a messenger from God, I suspect that we too would be afraid. The angel told him not to be afraid, because the messenger had been sent to let him know that his prayer had been heard and that his wife would bear him a son. Gabriel also told him that they were to name their son John. To say that Zechariah was skeptical, might be a bit of an understatement. Surely he had prayed for a son; they both had. Also he loved the sound of being a father to a son and he did not need to be told that a son would bring great joy to them.

Zechariah certainly lived his life to follow the God he loved, but this news from God's messenger brought to the forefront an area where his faith was beginning to falter. It was not that his faith in God faltered, but his faith in the truthfulness of God's messenger was lacking. So, because of his disbelief in the words of the angel Gabriel, Zechariah was struck mute. He was unable to speak until the child was born and they had named him John. The interesting thing was that when Zechariah came out from the altar area where he had burned the incense, the congregation gathered in the temple seemed to know that had happened to him. They assumed that because he had been in the sanctuary for so long and had been struck mute he must have seen a vision from God.

Later in the chapter, when John was born, friends and family gathered on the eighth day for his circumcision. Apparently the rabbi who was to do the circumcision assumed that they would want to name this long awaited son after his father. but Elizabeth said, "No; he is to be called John." Clearly that news was so unexpected that they looked to Zechariah to affirm or deny that decision. He motioned for a writing tablet and wrote, "His name is John." As soon as he had done that his ability to speak was restored. He began to praise God for all that God had done in their lives.

The people in attendance were amazed at what had happened and wondered what John might become. Clearly they believed that God's hand was upon him. Their suspicions were confirmed as Zechariah gave his prophesy concerning Israel and his son's role in helping to prepare the way for the Messiah. He would provide knowledge of salvation by forgiving their sins. Luke then said that John grew and became strong in spirit, but that he also stayed in the wilderness until he was ready to appear publicly in Israel.

We hear nothing more of John until Chapter 3, where he began his public ministry. His description shows him to be quite eccentric. All those years in the wilderness have obviously shaped his persona and his dietary selections. John was on a mission to help prepare Israel to receive their long=awaited Messiah. John's message was one of repentance and he baptized people to wash away their sin. Unlike the baptism of the Holy Spirit, which Jesus instituted, John's baptism had to be done repeatedly. It was symbolic of the washing away of sins, but persons would return to him to be washed again each time they felt convicted of their sinfulness again.

What is truly fascinating in John's story is that his call came before he was born and apparently, his parents reared him to grow into that call in such a way that he prepared himself for service to the people of Israel. Some of the people who heard him and were baptized by him thought he might be the Messiah, but he was quick to say that he was trying to prepare the people to ready to receive their Messiah when he did show up.

One of the things that John's story teaches us it that God always fulfills promises. John's story is one of a fulfilled promise to his aging parents. It also serves as a testimony to the fulfillment of God's promise to send a Messiah. These promises assure us that God always can be counted on to follow through with promises. The fact that we might have doubts about what God can do through us is just further affirmation that we are all in need of a Savior. While the people of Israel had been waiting for a Messiah for centuries, it did happen according to God's timing.

1. What can we learn from Zechariah's faith that we can apply to our own life?

2. Does it bring us any hope that even a priest, like Zechariah, could question God's surprising promise given the his and Elizabeth's ages?

3. Is a part of your sense of call related to expectations that your parents placed upon you or tried to help you live into as John's parents did for him?

4. What other details of the call of John stands out in your mind?

5. Do you see any similarities between John's story and your own?

MODERN DAY CALL STORY: MICHELLE BROWN

A Call to Teach By Michelle Brown

In second grade, when my teacher, Ms. T, pulled a disruptive student's desk to the back of the classroom, I thought, "That's gonna make it worse. She should move Donna next to Tish." And because I was an unmedicated kid with ADHD, I told her. That year, I would frequently pepper Ms. T with helpful suggestions, and after being shushed, notes on scraps of paper, giving her my insights on how to improve her craft. In fact, I coached many teachers throughout elementary, though none were in such dire need as poor Ms. T.

I got two school desks for my thirteenth birthday. Thirteen. School desks. Weird.

In middle school, I baby sat practically every weekend and took books to read to the children that included enrichment activities.

We'll skip over high school.

Until CPYC. It was at CPYC that I discovered myself. It was clear and with joy that I knew I was being called to teaching.

I declared my education major as a freshmen in college.

My first job application for Memphis City Schools asked for my school preferences. I left that blank, requesting only to be sent to an area with a low-economic population. When I was assigned to Dunbar Elementary in Orange Mound, I knew it was where God wanted me to be. The building was being renovated after having been closed for 7 years, and I would drive by every day to see how things were progressing. When I stood on the lawn, it felt like holy ground. My principal met me for the first time as I was climbing a wall to look in one of the classrooms. She later assigned me that room. My thirteen years there were special and challenging. I saw God almost every day. Until I didn't. I became a dry sponge, feeling my work was in vain. Students who had left my kindergarten class with such promise appeared to be demoralized and dejected by 5th grade. Despite having answered my call to follow God! I began to feel resentful toward my colleagues for not doing more, which led to anger and bitterness. God called me somewhere else.

It was sheer happenstance that I wound up at New Hope Christian Academy. It involved a chance meeting, a timely sermon, and a second chance meeting. So, I went. Though I met and worked with some amazing people, it was an overall dissatisfying experience. I felt like I'd deserted my people. I was a fierce supporter and believer of public schools. Why had I mistaken this as a calling? As soon as my two year contract was up, I put in my notice and applied to Memphis City Schools again.

Where did I wind up? Snowden School. Where I had attended years previously. Where my girls would attend. With teachers who nurtured me and challenged my craft. Where change and growth and learning is evident every day. I would never have left Dunbar for Snowden. It would've felt like selling out. But I could return to the public schools from an independent school. God knew my teaching was souring in Orange Mound. In order for me to continue, I'd need new wineskins.

I still dream about Dunbar. I feel regrets at not having been able to have remained vibrant and hopeful. That's my failing. But God made a way for me to continuing to answer my call as faithfully as I could.

After 27 years of teaching, there's not a day I dread going to work. As I tell my students, "There's no place I'd rather be than right here with you right now." That joy, that rightness, that contentment happens in the midst of some chaos and frustration sometimes. But I believe that passion and satisfaction will continue until my last teaching day.

1. What stands out to you in Michelle's call story?

2. Does anything in her story resonate with your own?

3. What do you think about the way that Michelle spoke of sensing that it was time to move on from her first teaching assignment?

4. As Michelle was leaving her second teaching assignment, she wondered if she had misunderstood God's call to that school. How do you feel about the notion that we may experience times when we feel as though we have misunderstood God's direction for our call?

5. What do you find affirming or challenging in Michelle's call story?

PROJECT

By now you should have a working plan for your project and you should be clarifying your desired goals and hoped outcomes. If you and your mentor need to spend time fine-tuning your project, by all means, you should do that. If you have already begun your project, you might spend some time talking about how it is going and see if you need to make any adjustments in your project plans.

OCTOBER

SUNDAY	MONDAY	TUESDAY
		1
6	7	8
13	14	15
20	21	22
27	28	29

FOCUS

WEDNESDAY	THURSDAY	FRIDAY	SATURDAY
2	3	4	5
9	10	11	12
16	17	18	19
23	24	25	26
30	31		

_____

_____

_____

_____

_____

_____

BIBLICAL CALL STORY: I SAMUEL 3

In order to talk about Samuel's call story, it might be helpful to remind yourselves of the beginning of Samuel's life. Samuel was the child of Elkanah and Hannah. Actually Elkanah had two wives, the other being Peninnah. Hannah was childless, but Peninnah had children and she liked to mock Hannah as a childless woman. This family traveled to Shiloh once a year to offer a sacrifice to the Lord. Elkanah noticed how sad Hannah was and tried to convince her that his love for her was not diminished by her barrenness. He gave her a double portion after he made the sacrifice, but Hannah wept and refused to eat. Hannah went to present herself and her distress before the Lord in the temple. She prayed and wept in the Temple moving her lips but making no sound. She promised God that if he would just give to her a son, she would give that child back to God to work in the temple.

Eli, the priest, saw her as she was praying and crying; he accused her of being drunk. She defended herself by saying that she had not any strong drink, but was pleading with God to hear her desire for a son. She also told him that she had promised to give that son back to God, if only God would answer her prayer. Eli blessed her with peace and that God would answer her petition. She went back to Elkanah greatly relieved and as they shared a meal, he could tell that she was no longer sad. When they returned home, Hannah became pregnant and gave birth to a son. She named him Samuel, because she had asked him of the Lord.

The next year when the family went to Shiloh, Hannah did not go with them. She told her husband that she would not return to Shiloh until her son was weaned, because she intended to give him to God for him to serve the Lord forever. Perhaps one of the surprising parts of this story is that Elkanah said, "Do what seems best to you." I cannot help but think that after all of the years of barrenness, Elkanah might have been a bit concerned that if Hannah did give her son back to God, she might return to her sad and miserable state from before. This would be a potentially difficult thing think that his beloved wife could give away that one son, but Elkanah agree to it. After Samuel was weaned, Hannah did take him to Shiloh and offered him to Eli to work in the temple. Hannah showed Eli that her prayer and his blessing had worked and as a result of that she was giving her son back to God to work in the temple. We also learn in the earlier part of Samuel's story that Elkanah and Hannah were blessed with three more sons and two daughters because of Hannah's sacrifice of giving Samuel to God.

Now in the text for this month we read about Samuel's call from God. It is important to note that Samuel received his call from God when he was still a boy working in the temple. The author said that the Word of the Lord was rare in those days. Eli was resting in his room and Samuel was lying down in the temple near the ark of the covenant. Even though Samuel was working in the temple, it seems surprising that he would be resting near the ark of the covenant, because the Holy of Holies was reserved for only priests. Samuel was clearly not yet a priest at his young age, yet he was allowed to be in there. While he was resting he heard someone call his name. Assuming that it was Eli, the boy went to him and asked what he wanted. Eli said that he did not call out Samuel's name. After the boy came to him the third time, Eli realized that it must have been the voice of God that Samuel was hearing.

He encouraged Samuel to stay where he was the next time that he heard his name and to say, "Speak, Lord, your servant is listening." Samuel did as he was told. The Lord delivered a message of rebuke against Eli's sons. This had to have been a difficult message to hear, because no one wants to tell a father that God is about to punish his household. The next morning when Eli awakened, he wanted a full report of what the Lord had said to Samuel. Samuel hesitated, because it was not happy news. Eli insisted that Samuel tell him the whole of God's prophecy. He did not want any detail left out and he told Samuel that anything he withheld from Eli should be done to him as well. Samuel told Eli everything that God had said to him in spite of the bad news that it was for Eli's family. Eli accepted the news by affirming that God must do whatever seems acceptable from God's perspective. Imagine the courage it would take for a boy to deliver such difficult news to his mentor and teacher. Samuel grew up and was seen as a trustworthy servant of the Lord, who continued to reveal himself to Samuel at Shiloh.

1. Have you ever wondered if Samuel resented his mother's decision to give him back to God at such an early age?

2. How might you feel if you sensed that others were pushing toward a call you may or may not feel ready to answer at this point in your life?

3. What do you hear or see in Samuel's call story that might influence your own sense of call?

4. In this story, Samuel's parents were not only supportive of his work for the Lord, but they initiated his call. How important is it to have the support of family and friends as you make the decision to follow the call of God in your life?

5. How much harder would it be to answer God's call, if a person felt that God's call would be difficult to do because it would involve sharing a message that others would not want to hear?

6. Does the fact that Samuel was so young when he heard the call of God impact the way that you feel about your own sense of call?

PROJECT

By now you should definitely be working on your project. You and your mentor need to spend some time talking about how it is progressing. You need to see if any modifications to your original plan might be helpful.

NOTES

NOVEMBER

GOALS

FOCUS

SUNDAY	MONDAY	TUESDAY
3	4	5
10	11	12
17	18	19
24	25	26

_____

_____

_____

_____

_____

WEDNESDAY	THURSDAY	FRIDAY	SATURDAY
		1	2
6	7	8	9
13	14	15	16
20	21	22	23
27	28	29	30

_____

_____

_____

_____

_____

_____

BIBLICAL CALL STORY: ABRAHAM, GENESIS 12:1-9; 15:1-6,18-21

The call of Abraham is one of the most significant call stories in the Bible. It came to a man from Haran who was a nomad, traveling from one piece of pasture land to another in order to provide food for his flocks and herds. There is no indication that he was a follower of Yahweh before he received his call. As a matter of fact, there were gods worshiped by nomads to protect them and provide for them along their journeys. These were likely the gods that Abraham worshiped. But when God called to Abraham to take a faith journey to a place that God would make known to him in time, Abraham was willing to gather up his belongings and his people to depart on the journey.

The interesting thing about this otherwise unremarkable event is that Christians and Jews both believe that, in this one story, we see a turning point for all humans and even for the totality of creation. There are many things special about this particular call, not the least of which is the fact that, like all call stories, God takes the initiative to call Abraham. God chose this man and his family to be the starting point of the covenant to form a people who would be blessed not just for themselves, but for the sake of helping all of the rest of humankind back to their true home with God. Both Christians and Jews see this story as the beginning of God's story of redemption and salvation. Jews still look to Abraham as the father of the faithful. Christians see him as that, but also see Jesus as the completion and fulfillment of that covenant.

If Abraham had not responded to this call from God in the way that he did, our faith story might be drastically different. It was through Abraham that God's relationship with Israel was initiated. The shocking thing about this story is that this covenant with Abraham was like a reset button on human history. One of the puzzling things in this story is that Abraham, who was 75 years old and childless at the time he heard God's call, believed that God could make him the father of a great nation, with more descendents than he or anyone else could count. Why might he have been willing to accept that call?

It helps to remember who Abraham was. He was fairly low on the societal ladder in his culture, as nomadic people often are. He and his wife were old enough that they had basically given up hope of ever having children of their own. With little hope of children and little hope of a permanent place to call home, Abraham was just the kind of person who might be willing to hear this call from God a great opportunity to change his circumstances. People who are that near to being hopeless are often better able to hear such a call than those who are more settled and stable.

We need to remember that, in the ancient world, one's family or tribe would help one another to survive during challenging times. Knowing that, we might think that Abraham's family might have been less than thrilled when they learned that he was about to depart for another place. He had flocks and herds, which could help to sustain the entire tribe if times got tough. We also might wonder if Sarah and Lot were as thrilled about this move or if they tried to dissuade him of this journey, especially if he was honest with them about what had prompted him to make this journey in the first place. They might have questioned his willingness to travel to an unspecified location at the request of the Living God, whom they did not recognize as their own. Did they know that God had invited Abraham on a journey without fully disclosing where they would end up staying? Or were they just so accustomed to the nomadic life that they never really questioned where they were going when setting out on any journey?

We must remember that God promised three things to Abraham in this call. God promised a land which would be show to him in time. God promised Abraham descendants who would grow into a great nation. Then God promised him a special blessing which would provide protection from opponents for him and future generations in addition to the opportunity to bless all people throughout the earth because of their blessings. One might speculate that the first two blessings alone might have been enough, but the third one might have sweetened the pot a little.

When Abraham, Sarah and Lot arrived in Canaan, God said something very important that we might have missed on our first reading of this passage. In verse 7, God said, "To your offspring I will give this land." Notice God did not say, "To you, I will give this land." That might have been Abrahams first clue that though God's promise could be counted upon, Abraham might not live long enough to see it come to full fruition. As we know from looking at the rest of the Abraham story, the total fulfillment of those promises did not come before his death. Perhaps this is why Abraham has been called the pioneer of the faith, because he believed that those promises would be fulfilled even if it was not to be in his lifetime.

In Genesis 15, it is clear that Abraham is showing some concern about the fact that he and Sarah are still childless. His despair over not having a child is weighing on him. He does not want a slave to be his only heir, but that was the situation at that point in his story. Again God assures him that he and Sarah will indeed have more offspring than the number of stars in the sky. Clearly that means that the number of their descendants will be too many to actually count. And again, Abraham believed God's promise and God reckoned that to him as righteousness. Note that again in Chapter 15, God told him that the land would be given to his descendants in future generations, but that he would die in peace knowing that God's promise to Abraham's descendants would ultimately be fulfilled.

Abraham's faith remained strong in spite of the fact that he and Sarah had only one child. They believed that God would make their descendants many and that God would fulfill all of the promises in that initial call story. Yes, God needed to repeat the promises from time to time in order to assure Abraham and Sarah, but even when they questioned, they believed that God to do what God had promised. They just seemed to question God's timing a bit.

1. What stands out to you in Abraham's call story?

2. What do you think of the notion that God's call can be more easily heard by those who are hopeless or in dire straits?

3. Can you identify with any part of Abraham's call story?

4. What do you think about Abraham's willingness to follow God on the journey of faith without knowing exactly where that journey might lead him?

5. How might God's call on your life be a call to participate in a journey of faith with God?

6. What do you think about the notion that God's promises to Abraham were not fulfilled in his lifetime?

7. Does any part of Abraham's call story frighten you or comfort you?

Take time to reflect on your experience.

NOTES

DECEMBER

GOALS

FOCUS

SUNDAY	MONDAY	TUESDAY
1	2	3
8	9	10
15	16	17
22	23	24
29	30	31

_____

_____

_____

_____

_____

WEDNESDAY	THURSDAY	FRIDAY	SATURDAY
4	5	6	7
11	12	13	14
18	19	20	21
25	26	27	28

_____

_____

_____

_____

_____

Jonah is one of the most striking examples from the Bible of a heart in need of expansion. God called, but Jonah ran.

Miraculously he survived not only being thrown into the storm tossed ocean but he even survived being swallowed whole by a large fish. He remained in the belly of that fish for three days. While in the fish, Jonah prayed to the Lord, thanking him for his protection. After the three days and nights, the fish vomited Jonah back onto dry land unscathed.

Then, Jonah did what the Lord asked of him: He traveled to Nineveh, an enemy of the Israelites, to proclaim the Lord's judgment. The Ninevites almost immediately repented and were shown mercy by the Lord. The book ends with Jonah brooding over Nineveh, angry that his worst fear had been realized. He did not think that God should have extended grace to the people Jonah so despised. As a matter of fact, one of the reasons that he tried to go to Tarshish was because he did not want his warning of judgment to convince the Ninevites to repent. He knew that if they heeded his warning, God would surely be merciful and forgive them.

On the surface, Jonah seems to be a melodramatic and fearful man who begrudgingly obeyed God's will and—in a surprising narrative twist—was actually angry when he was successful at his task. But to truly understand Jonah's bitterness and fear, it is important that we understand what Jonah was facing when God told him to go to Nineveh. During this time period, the Ninevites were not only enemies of the Israelites but had violently oppressed the nation of Israel. God's command for Jonah, therefore, was not just unreasonable. It was terrifying, because the realistic expectation for a Jew going among the people of Nineveh would be to put one's self at risk of great personal danger. Not to mention that fact that a Jew convincing Ninevites of anything seemed impossible, at best.

These cultural realities were most likely a huge part of why Jonah ran from God's will boarding a ship bound for Tarshish in the first place. He was naturally terrified of this real enemy. Maybe he could also have been afraid of failure. The very thought of proclaiming God's judgment to an enemy nation is a overwhelming. Perhaps Jonah figured the odds of the Ninevites heeding God's command were too small for him to risk his very life and also perhaps his dignity.

At the core of Jonah's fears, though, there was something much deeper at work: the fear of triumph. Jonah knew that, if he succeeded at winning over the Ninevites to the Lord, they would be shown mercy. Jonah knew about the way God works: He shows his abundant grace to undeserving people. Jonah, on the other hand, wanted his enemies to suffer. He may well have been concerned that his fellow Jews would be upset with him if the Ninevites did heed his warning and turn their lives toward God. Would his peers have felt that he had betrayed his community by helping their enemy?

After Jonah was spit out of the mouth of the great fish, he again heard the word of the Lord concerning his call to go to Nineveh. This time he did go to Nineveh. He proclaimed the message that Nineveh would be overthrown in 40 days. Nineveh was a huge city which took him three days to walk across. The people of Nineveh heeded his warning and even the king ordered a decree that all of Nineveh was supposed to fast and sit in sackcloth and ashes in order to repent for their wicked ways. the king wanted not only the people to observe this fast but even their animals. He also ordered the people to cry out to God for mercy. Jonah's fears had come to fruition.

Isn't it strange that Jonah felt called to a task that he did not want to do. So, he hoped that God would not make his efforts pay off for Nineveh. He actually did not want to succeed in his task. As a matter of fact, he was angry with God for showing mercy and extending grace to the people of Nineveh. He was so angry that he asked God to take his life from him, not just once, but twice. He deemed that he was better off dead than alive. God clearly did not agree to that request. Instead, God tried to teach Jonah a lesson about God's grace and mercy. One of the beautiful affirmations in this text is that God cares for the Godless and the corrupt and simply desires that all people and all nations turn to God.

Think about the irony that Jonah could have died after being thrown overboard, but by God's mercy he was saved by becoming fish food. Granted that experience might have felt a little like a mixed blessing. And though Jonah was thankful that his life had been spared, he could not see that this God of second chances should want to offer a second chance for the people of Nineveh.

1. What stands out to you in Jonah's call story?

2. Does anything surprise you in Jonah's story?

3. Do you see any similarities between his call story and your own?

4. Do you see similarities between Jonah's call and any of the other call stories that we have studied?

5. Have you ever tried to run from God's call in your life?

6. Why might you be afraid to answer God's call?

7. Jonah continued to receive grace from God to the very end of his story. In what ways have you been a recipient of God's grace or how have you witnessed grace in others around you?

8. What actions or attitudes do you need to change so that others can see Jesus more clearly in your life?

Take time to reflect on your experience.

NOTES

www.ingramcontent.com/pod-product-compliance
Lightning Source LLC
Chambersburg PA
CBHW041053110426

42740CB00044B/48